==I have spent more than 24yrs in the prison system of the state of Illinois; I have met and exchanged with the intellectual giants of the prison system. Men such as, Mo-dee-bo, Jerome (Bones) Davis, Johnny (Kenyatta El) Miles, Louis Rosa, Johnny Ray Stone El. Michael Brooks Bey, Vampoon, Reginald Morgan Bey, John lee Lipscomb Bey, Minister Michael X, The Christian Brother Named Moses. There are so many brothers of the prison system. Who was instrumental in shaping my perspective, on History, Religion, political science, Civil and Criminal Law; These are the men of the prison system who exchanged books, and argument on the subjects named above, which gave me my foundation, and formed my opinion of what a Man is. I was, taught by these men, that Men who championed, the cause of our peoples here in the Diaspora, unselfishly, were the men, to follow. Exposed to such notable, scholar as, Dr. Ben Jochanna, in his many works, Ian van Sertama, Dr. John Hedrick Clark, Diop, Chancellor William, J.A. Rogers, Godfrey Higgins, Albert Churchward, C.F. Volney, Kersey Graves, Noble Drew Ali, Marcus Garvey, Davis walker, Nat Turner, Denmark Vesey, Gabriel Posey etc. To me these men are prophets, they are the only men to bring a pure and clear message of liberation to the African, all over the world. None of these men brought a message or doctrine, advocating the enslavement, of their fellow humans. I did not find among the African prophets, their equals in the bible, or the prophets spoken of in the Quran. I was unable to find Abrahams Equal, among the African, because there is no records of any of these prophet marrying their sisters. I was unable to find David's equal, because they are not noted for having a man murdered, because you slept with his wife. Samson, was not found either among, the African prophets in the Diaspora, I was not able to find any, which could be labeled a serial killer and a robber. Neither was Elijah found, nor, were Lot found. Even in the mythology of the ancient world, there are not records of a prophet, of god, having sex, with his two, daughter, to perpetuate his race. I learned in the course of time, that the things said of, and suggested by these men of the bible, is amoral. Consequently, whenever I had a platform in which to speak, this is what I taught, which the teachers named above taught me, throughout the prison system for more than 17yrs. I taught Religion and history from a Afro-Centric prospective. It is from these lessons, and experiences, and my common sense that I have arrived at this conclusion of what a man is. Moreover, these are my conclusions.

A man is one who meets the challenges, of Nature and prevails. Can you imagine the Magnitude of these challenges, facing the first man? The first example, we have of man challenges of nature, are, the first example given by the African man and woman of the Nile Valley. Here the forces of the universe, was against them, and they overcame and survived. First, they tamed the wild beast and domesticated, livestock's, the African man and woman, equally contributing, realized the need for shelter, and the importance of gathering food. Here in this atmosphere, Religion, Mathematic and Medicine was realized, astrology, Astronomy, (the first stellar calendar at this point is over 10.000 years old,) Physic, Engineering, (These African with their vast knowledge of the sciences, are responsible for putting the "S" shape in the Nile River) Endogamy and Exogamy. See: Black man of The Nile and his family, by Dr. Yusuf Ben Johanna, and Signs and Symbols of Primordial Man, by Albert Churchward. Here alone the banks of this River in Africa are Man root. It is, now agreed, and acknowledged by, the so-called scientific communities that, the African man and woman, are the first of the human race on earth. Moreover, this man and woman, have a very dark pigmented skin. He was the first of the human race, and they are the first of the human family, existing in sub-tropical Africa. This first man is the man directly from God, the only one, every other man (Race) came thru this man, (this is so in myth, or reality.) Moreover, these are the ones that, we see with their human industry, up and down the Nile valley,

culminating in the high cultures of Egypt. However, Egypt is the youngest of the Africans High Culture, According to Dr. Ben and Dr. John Henry Clark and Ivan Van- Sertima, Ethiopia and Nubians, are older than Egypt. Before any of these African high culture came into existence, the African had already subdued the Earth and Mapped out the Heavens with precision. In These High Cultures Nubia, Ethiopia, and Egypt, Africans perfected the art of writing, and built Monuments and, erected temples, and spanned the globe leaving evidence of his relics. He introduced Civilization to the Rest of Humanity, in fact, the African Race, after bringing forth humanity, is the only race of humanity to practice civilization, all other races practice aggression toward the African, First the Hysso, Then, the Persian and Greeks, and the Romans and Muslims. These entire nation practiced aggression, against their African Fathers. Nevertheless, the African had already developed their High Culture, before there was any foreign invasion. Egypt, at this point in history is more than, Four thousand years older, than the Adam and Eve story. The pyramids, and the sphinx, are already constructed and more than 13 dynasties old. Before there was a Abraham, and where are Moses, and Muhammad? Well, they are not born yet! (How sad it is for Islam to clam that, the belief in the one god, was not complete, until the Qur'an was, given to Muhammad.) Already Akhenaton is preaching the belief in the one God, this is happening thousands of years before there is a man named Abraham. However, the belief in the one God is not the only religion practiced by the African, as we shall see; The African of the Nile Valley are the first of the human race, to have a belief based on the trinity concept. Dr. Ben summed up the trinity concept as follows;"Mommy, Daddy, and Me". At this point in history, there was not a Male God without his Female consort. In all of the African societies of antiquity, there are Goddesses. In fact, man first god was a goddess,   in the Egyptian religion, and all of the African societies, up and down the Nile, they worshipped the Goddesses Nut, and Mut, Isis, Hator etc. (Moreover, this concept, of reverence for motherhood stems from the high regards, and high honors given to the woman, in Africans societies. The two are represented everywhere, in Egyptian culture. Before there was a Mary, and Jesus concept, it was believe by the African of the Nile Valley that, The Goddess Isis was the mother of the god Horus. Horus, Isis, and Osiris, represents the trinity in the Egyptian pantheon. This is thousands of years before it was said, "Holy Mary Mother of God". The Nile Valley Africans also had a belief in Death, and Resurrection. Moreover, in this belief Horus, the Sun god is the first, of the World Savior, to be crucified. He died, and conquered death and resurrected, on the third Day! See Africa the Mother of Civilization by Dr. Yusuf Ben Jochanna. See also, Kersey Graves, The world Sixteen Crucified Saviors. The Africans of the Nile Valley also had forty-two laws, called the negative confession. In biblical and qu'ranic history Moses are known for having ten of these negative confessions, of the African of the Nile Valley; they are called the Ten Commandments. In addition, the Proverbs of David has been determined to be, the writing of Pharaoh Amen-e-o-pe. These saying, attributed to King David of Israel, are called the Proverbs. They are the Word for Word Saying of Pharaoh Amen-o-pe. Islam, as practiced by the Arabs, Validates the claim of the Old and new testament, that David is the author of the proverbs, biblical and Qu'ranic writer didn't count on us uncovering this lie, but let's look at the above lie, and the ones to follow. God is the truth, so he should be telling the truth, in his revealed books. The statement above, clearly shows that not only is it a lie, that David, is the author of the Proverbs, they also clearly states that the Jews were slaves in Egypt and they was forced to build the pyramids. Both of these lies are found in the books of the three religions Judaism, Christianity, and Islam. Relic of the African man and woman, are found all over the earth. Wherever there is human industry, evidence of the African is there. His presence is noted, in Monument and temple building. There is evidence of him, in India, Japan, Europe, the Americas, etc. There is no evidence, of a High Culture in these lands, prior to the coming of the African. Equally said; there is not any evidence of a human being on the earth, prior to the Coming of the African, Moreover, it is the same with religion, Medicine, Math, Writing, Planned Parenthood, etc. there is no human example of these, before the example given by the Man, and Woman of Africa. Using true history as our guide, we shall see that the concept of God originated with the African, and so did the Concept of" Honor Thy Mother, and Thy Father. Just as in creation, there is no example of creation, before the example given by God. Or in other words, there is no example of creation, given before that first example, I simply call it God, and God to me is defined as the Originator, the First: Likewise, with the human family, The Godhead in the African Society has always been, Mother and Father, The first human being, these are, the Gods on Earth. Moreover, they had many gods come from them. We call them races, but only god can produce God. That is why in the Egyptian Pantheon. The African understood that the act of procreation could not be, without these two, mommy, and daddy! Only human can produce human. The African man understood that a greater, importance was attached to the mother, because she carried and nurture life, and brought it to conception. That is why she has always, been revered as the mother of god, BECAUSE SHE IS! However, this does not diminish the importance of the father. They realized that they were co-equal, and this is reflected in all of their temples and monument. The Pharaohs and Queen is, always shown reigning over the Egyptian empire jointly. Which is symbolic of mother, and father, they are defined as Gods, the one who originates here on earth. It is misleading, and delusional, for man to think, that he is born into creation, and he is the maker, thereof. Likewise, it is so with humanity, it is delusional for any race of peoples to lay claims to being the first gods (race of peoples) on earth. Delusions do not change the fact, facts remains, and delusions dissipate. The Egyptian claims that," they came from the beginning of the Nile, where God Hapi dwells". They understood their origin, and gave honors to their Mothers and fathers, who dwell at the foothill of the mountains at the foothills of the moon, in Africa. Moreover, where do we find the most accomplished human effort toward the formation and development of the law, which will govern human society, pre-Ethiopia, Nubian, Egypt? There is nothing anterior to this man effort, because there is no other man, so all of these accomplishments must be his. Just like there is nothing anterior to God's initiative, and creation is solely and exclusively his initiative, then likewise it is so with man and his initiatives, Mathematics, Science, religion, Moral and civil law, etc. How can anyone, with a foundation build on these, be the originator of these? Can man, who is the created, truly say that he is the creator? Neither can any man, or race, lay claims to being the originator of any of the discipline named above. Just as with god, there can only be one originator, and there is nothing new under the sun! Seemingly, the story of the first Man and his providence parallel the story of God and Stan; God according to the narrative, originated the essence of everything, including the nature of Satan. Moreover, Satan sought to usurp God as Originator. Satan is delusional! You can never be the maker of the god, who made you. Neither can the sons, ever be the father, of the father. Likewise, man and his descendants had similar trials, because the children's of the African from Asia, (for the sake of clarity) sought to overthrow the kingdom of their parents. (Can the geographical location of one birth, by itself change the nature of a man decent line?) Can culture or topography standing by themselves, change the nature of his descent? Then something else must have happen to cause the African to regard his offspring's, in Asia, as something separate and distinct, from themselves. What happen, why are their descendants, referred to as humankind? We know that the descendants, of the African, left Africa. So clearly, they were migratory, and there are many human afflictions and infirmities associated with gregarious migratory groups, See Ian Van Sertima, the African Presence in early Europe. Also, see, Signs and symbols of Primordial Man, by Albert Churchward. Albinism is one of these afflictions; if Albinism, alone with topography and diet, were a consideration, this would explain the Africans, referring to his descendants as humankind. These are they (Just as Satan was, in god kingdom) within the African kingdom, who sought to overthrow their Mothers and Fathers. Abraham is the chief of these, who lead the attack. Just as Satan, was the chief rebel, in god's kingdom, leading the attack? Moreover, Satan had many followers, who titles are Lucifer, devil, dragon and beast, Satan is the first. He is described as, a liar and a cheat, claiming, that he was made to build the pyramids, and that god overthrew the Egyptian, because of their enslavement, of the

Hebrews, etc. so he must be liken, to the Hyssos invasion, of their Mother, and Fathers heavenly paradise, (Africa). Next, it was Cambyses of Persia, who I liken to Lucifer, the Devil is Alexander the great of Greece, the Dragon is Rome, Under Julius Caesar, and the Beast is America, Under George Washington. These are the children's of the Africans, who came back to Africa with the intent, to overthrow their Mother and Fathers, kingdom. Moreover, there is one son not yet named, but we see him clearly, and his name is Judaism, Christianity, and Islam. He is the aberrant one. With these came Death, and devastations; slavery, and everything that harm followed these. Now the African, man and woman, who started this completely human process, is now captive, and taught that he did nothing at all to advance civilization. He is taught that, his Prophets, and Holy Men are criminal, and crooks. Moreover, that his Captors, the Master enslavers and murderer, George Washington, and the other so call founding fathers, of America are his heroes. He knows absolutely nothing about the nature of his captors, and believes him to be a friend, a brother! The only knowledge he have, is what his captors has taught him. He knows absolutely nothing, of his glorious past. He knows nothing of his divine kinship, with the original God; in fact, he does not know that he is a god. He does not know that as God, he was the first to subdue and tame the earth, because his captors are telling him, that others did it. He forgot the precept "Man know yourself" He is not aware of the importance of family, because this knowledge was bred out of him. These last episodes of a combined force from, Judaism, Christianity, and Islam, has endured concertedly for, more than five hundred years, on the psychic of the African and teaches, him, against himself. Consequently, He does not know that it was he, who conquered Spain in 711, Portugal, and southern France. These African called themselves, Moors. The Moors were defeated in 1493 A.D after ruling Spain, Portugal, and Southern France for more than seven hundred years. Following this defeat, the Moors, at the behest of Bishop Bartholomew De La Casa, to the pope, were sent to the Island of Hispaniola; today the name for Hispaniola is Haiti. These Moors was brought there as slaves, and these are the first, of the African to be enslaved in the Americas. The Children of Arabia are the first, in the history of humankind, to introduce chattel slavery to the African continent, the home, of their Mothers, and Fathers. The Arabs had this practice of enslaving in chattel, six hundred years before their European counterpart. See Chancellor Williams, The Destruction of Black Civilization. Look at the horrors this episode, of man inhumanity to man entails. No, let us consider them collectively. One hundred Millions African died, during this episode of man's history, the worst example, of man inhumanity, to man. However, the Africans are, taught that the only holocaust that really matters, is the one that happen during Hitler's reign. Therefore, he does not know that, no people have ever, sustained a loss of 100 millions peoples, and lived.

He does not realize that he is yet suffering from that loss. The Jews, do not tell that their Prophet Moses, instructed them to exterminate completely the Midanites,"Save the women alive, and kill everything that pisses against the wall", but the African is taught to honor this because it is said, the God of the Jews sanctioned it. I cannot agree, Holocaust, No! I refuse to share this platform, with any member of the human race, past, or present, claiming such! Just this act alone impresses me that Judaism, Christianity, and Islam as practice by the respective groups, are of the dens of Satan. Any religion suggesting the enslavement of any people is demonic. The god's and prophets of the above named religion, all sanction slavery, and makes it a perpetual condition. There are no words to properly, describe slavery. The only description that I can give of Slavery is that it is an institution of horror. Moreover, the gods of the scriptures of Judaism, Christianity, and Islam, issued instructions for the slave to be contented with his Lot. "Servants be obedience to you master in all things pertaining to the flesh" is this suppose to justify the raping of Women's, and the killing of innocence?) Many of these Africans refused to accept, the perpetual state of his condition, and revolted. These revolts, was lead by such notable Prophets as, David Walker, Denmark Vesey, Gabriel Poser. In his book, David Walker's Appeal, he had this to say as far back as 1829,"having traveled over a considerable portion of these united states, and having, in the course of my travels, taken the most accurate observation of things as they exists, the result of my observation has warranted the unshakable conviction, that we (colored peoples of these united states.) are the most Wretched, and degraded, and abject set of being, to ever live, since the world began. And I pray to god, that none like us live again, until time shall be, no more. They tell us, of the Israelites, in Egypt, the Helot in Sparta, and of the Roman slaves, which, the last was made up, from almost every nation under the heavens, who suffered under those ancient and heathen nations, were in comparison, with ours, under this enlighten, and Christian nation, no more than a cipher,--or in other words, those heathen nations of antiquity, had but little among them than the name, and form of slavery. While wretchedness,' and endless miseries were reserved, apparently in a phial, to be poured out upon, our father, ourselves, and our children by the Christians of America". Further, he states" I, call upon the professing Christian, I, call upon the philanthropist, I, call upon the very tyrant himself to show me, one page, of history either sacred, or profane. On which a verse can be found, which maintains that the Egyptian, heaped the insupportable, insult upon the children's of Israel. By telling them, that they were not, of the human family". Can the whites, deny this charge? Have they not, after having reduced us, to the deplorable condition of slave, under their feet, held us up as originally descending from tribes of monkeys, orang-outangs? O My God, I appeal to every man of feeling,-is not this insupportable? Is it not heaping the most gross insults, upon our miseries? Because they have us under their feet, and we, cannot help ourselves? O Pity us I pray Lord Jesus, master, --has Mr. Jefferson Declared to the world that we are inferior, to the white, both in the endowments of our bodies, and mind? It is indeed surprising that a man of such great learning, combined with excellence natural parts, should speak so on a set of men in chains. I do not know, what to compare it to, unless, like putting one wild deer in a cage, where it will be secured, and hold another by the side of the same, then let it go ,and expecting the one in the cage, to run as fast as the one at liberty. So far, my brethrens were the Egyptian, from heaping these insults upon their slaves, that pharaoh daughter took Moses a son of Israel as her own. Mr. Walker farther stated, "Hear you own declaration American! Do you understand your own language? Proclaimed to the world July4th 1776, WE HOLD THESE TRUTH TO BE SELF EVIDENT---THAT ALL MEN ARE CREATED EQUAL! They are, endowed by their creator with CERTAIN UNALIENABLE RIGHTS; among these are life, liberty and the pursuit of happiness. compare your own language above, extracted from your declaration of independence, with your cruelties, and murders, inflicted by your cruel, and unmerciful fathers, and yourselves, upon our father and on us. Men who have never given you, or your fathers the slightest provocation! These men knew that if, their brethren knew better, they would do better. Moreover, unlike Moses, they did not wait until they were 85yrs old to champion, the cause of their peoples. Capture in an atmosphere of hate and violence, completely without the knowledge of self, or the rights of man. The freedom that he gave humanity is now denied him, the very sciences that he originated and gave to the world, is refused him. It is said that the highest height, are gained by those, who has reached the lowest depth, in this equation clearly, the African man and woman fell from the highest heights of God and Goddess ,King and Queen, to the level of a slave. Reflective in this saga, is the attributes of God the Absolute. The Heights that, the African man and woman, reached is matched only, by his lowest depth, slavery, which represent the completeness of the human being. Just as the totality, and completeness of existence, is representative of God the Absolute. So is the high and lows of man, the first man, is a representation of this attribute of God. This man is clearly God chosen, because he is the first god chose, to exhibit god like qualities, he tamed his environment to his purpose. Therefore, he is, the originator of these, and cannot share this platform with another, these are exclusively his, just as God distinction is exclusively his own, and he cannot share this platform with another. Goodness and love for humankind came from this man, it was love that causes him to stand upright and face the challenges before him, and it was this love, he extended to his descendants. Goodness, mercy, and love, came from this first man, made in the image and likeness of God. This original man did not ascend to the heights he attained, by stepping on the backs of his brethren, no;

wherever the African found his descendant, he extended love and goodwill. Never, in Africa, was a man taught that he was something other than himself. The three blows sustained to the head of Hiram Abiff, in Freemasonry, are the same as the three blows suffered by the African; these blows came from Judaism, Christianity, and Islam. However, there is only one master builder, and one great architect, none can replace him, so everyone needs to stop pretending, you can never be this man, because you cannot originate, no matter how much you pretend. Just as this man, could never be the absolute god, no matter how much he pretends. Because God is the first to, originate. Envy, jealousy and hate has always been the driving force behind the aggression against the African by their offspring's, i.e. humanity, what else can explain the atrocious and viciousness of the European, the Jews and the Arabs, toward their African fathers? We taught them, that a man has the right; to be secure in his home or property, without fear of molestation from his neighbor, and that society must be govern by Just law. See, C.F. Volney, Ruins of Empires But instead of applying the law as given by their parents, they introduced horrors unthinkable! Just as Satan, and his entourage, had done in the kingdom, of Yahweh. However, in that narrative, Satan was casted out, and we all know his ends. Envy was the sole motive, for the aggression of the children's, against their mother and fathers. Now this African Man and Woman, (the first of the gods and goddess) after suffering these blows, in the head by the three religions Judaism, Christianity, and Islam, are left wheeling without direction, and these three religions are the culprit. However, this is not the first challenges of this proportion to face the African Man. As stated above he overcame the force the universe threw at him and prevailed, now he is facing slavery, a form design specifically and exclusively for him, this is what distinguishes this man, from all of the other races, claiming that they also suffered enslavement. How they lie! They know that there is not a condition; suffered by any race of peoples, on equal footing with the slavery the African is yet subject too, never in the history of a people, have a people been so despised, and rejected, and thoroughly brainwashed against them self. No conquered nations, and enslaved peoples, of antiquity ever had their identity taken from them, to the point that he could not recognize his natural brother and sister. Even how, he should behave in defense of Father, Mother, Sons, Daughters, sister brother, family and Race, for fear of reprisals from his captors. Slavery endures time, as long as the slave believes that he is a slave, he is indeed a slave. Moreover, the only way to affect this in the human being is to instill docility into the minds of the children's, and this is introduced to the child consciousness thru terror and intimidation. These coupled with mis-education, robs the African man and woman of the knowledge of self. This is the fate of the African man and woman here in America, indeed around the world. African Kings, who do not realize, that they are kings, are seen daily, on the street corners, with their pant hanging, with a fish full of dope claiming, "I'm a Boss"! Moreover, the African Woman not knowing, that she is a true queen by nature, are seen daily, walking the street with buttocks showing, jumping in and out of cars with strange men, stripping and showing their body for dollars, the greatest insults to her father, she do, everyday. I ask you woman is this characteristic of a Queen? Black woman, when did any African queen, compromises her virtue for a pauper fee. Stop pretending, you are what you are, and your actions clearly shows it. If you are daily conducting yourself as a Harlot, then claim it; stop claiming that you are a queen, because a queen is more dignified. She would never willing give herself to her captor, for a fee, for any reason, to do so cannot distinguish her from any other Commoner. Because, she knows that, she is the giver and preserver of life. And she cautions her daughters against promiscuity, because she know that, activities such as these are frown upon, in all societies" The hand that rock the cradle raises the nation". You can never be a liberator sleeping with the enemy, never in the history of the slave, saga in American, did the white man exalt his black mistress, in public, above any white woman, no matter how wretched. Consequently, black man, and woman, you are wondering, why those of us, who feels strongly about your actions, look at you with contempt and disdain! It is because we know, that you are wretched, and is the dregs of society, and everyday your action shows it, you are the only one, deluded. Moreover, Black Man stop claiming that you are a Boss, A.K.A. King, how is this reflected in your everyday behavior? Where is the evidence that you are a man? Men do not allow other men to, over run their communities without opposition. They do not allow other men to rape their wives and daughters, and live! Dr. Ben stated, "Show me how you treat you woman, and I'll show you the condition of your race". What is it that grippes you black man, that you cannot act in your own best interest, or in defense of yourself? Is it ignorance's or fear? A combination of these two would explain why the African man and woman, in their present state of mind, are hell bent on destruction. The hand that rocks the cradle raises the nation. As stated above, your, example of motherhood, is compromised everyday by your very actions, you are renowned around the world as WHORE! How did you lose your distinction as Goddess, Queen, Mother, etc? A man idea is his god, You, African woman, are following another man's idea, and so is your man, but he is living what you taught him. How can you explain this to your son, when every day, this is what you do, and the whole world see it. Can you explain to him that years ago his father's lost the war, and has yet to recover? How can you explain to him that at one point, you reign as Queen supreme, and your delight now is to be a WHORE, WILL YOU TEACH HIM TO follow your example and revel in perversity? Your only solution is to cease from doing the things that gave you that distinction, in the first place. Wretched is your condition and no amount of compromising and making exception for, will cure it sufficiently to make it respectable. How can you teach him what you yourself do not know? You must teach him that freedom is not, earned on your knees begging. You cannot teach him liberation, lying in the master's bed, and he sees it; No! They have a name, for that kind of woman, and we all know it, but you. How deluded can you be? The hand that rocks the cradle raises the nation, if you cannot teach him anything, about how he should face the challenges of the world, and instead teach him to be passive, and docile toward his enemy, how do you think he is going to approach life. This is the underlying cause of most of the domestic cases in the black household, because most black men know how the black woman will regard him, measuring him, and his worth, against another man idea. Moreover, for her to bring her unsound reasons into the home, to justify her perverted ideas, adds further to his emasculations. He realizes that she cannot honor him truly as a man, because he is not! Men protect, and provide, and in this environment begging and assimilation is encouraged in him. The Blackman remain with her because he knows that without her he could not be. Now he's, without input or, authority in his own home, from his woman, because unwittingly she is complicit, in depriving him of it. He or she don't, understand that assimilation is fatalistic to the race, No race of peoples have ever honored a hybrid race, and this is what assimilation breeds, Hybrids are like Janus, you can never tell which face they are wearing. Begging is also fatal, because your livelihood is contingent upon the mercies of other. Assimilation is right and healthy in an environment, where races agree to assimilated, but this was not assimilation, this is miscegenation. Consequently, the African race in the Americas is an amalgamated race, left in total confusion, not knowing that, allegiance, is to himself first, and others secondly. I have a duty to my family and race, and the preservation of these first. Integration, Caused irreparable harm to us as a race of peoples. When segregated we had the greatest opportunity the universe could have given us to self heal. Although our enemy was present round about us, and was on his campaign of terror, we had the opportunity to self heal, as a group. When the Europeans powers, decided to give palatine, to the European Jews, (the white European Jew was a persecuted group, and no one is denying that.) As such, they understood that they needed isolation, from all other group of peoples, in order to teach their children the tragedy of what happen to them, and how they could prevent this from happening in the future. They, did not wait, or allow anyone to tell their story, or write their history. Not that I'm comparing the suffrages of the Jews with ours, no there is no comparison there, but there is much to be learned from the opportunity that we had when we were segregated. We had positive examples among us when segregated, we had doctor, lawyers, and engineers, ETC.TO EMULATE. Thus, we had accountability, the community was accountable to each other, and they understood that the bad actions of one reflected badly on the community as a whole. The pinnacles of, uncle, aunt, big cousin, had value, and none can deny the industrious act of the African in Tulsa Oklahoma, which was a beacon for the world(But once again envy, jealousy and hatred, of the African, by white America, destroyed these aspirations.) We were well on our way toward distinguishing ourselves, and realizing who we were as a people. Then came segregation, and the positive educated class of our peoples moved out of the community , leaving as their replacement, Pimps, Prostitute, drugs dealers, thugs, etc. Professions once frowned upon in our communities, is now glorified. Consequently, the positive, images, of the black doctors, lawyers, and businesspersons etc. was, replaced with negative images. and, the professional, and educated class, among our peoples sought assimilation, and a leave it to beaver life style, the farther they could get away from the black community, the more secured they felt, living the illusion that they were something different and distinct from those peoples. Is there any wonder then, that hopelessness reign on the face of our youth? They do not know who, or what, to belong to. His leadership has failed him completely; we need to teach ourselves, about our self and the world. This is the position taken by all men all over the world, but he don't know that because, he is not taught to think for himself, as other men think, he is taught to think as something less than a man, because he is taught against himself. He is taught as an individual, and consequently he is, taught what to think. This is reflected in his daily life, he does not see himself as a group, with common issues, from common foes. In fact, he does not see his enemy as a foe. Because he is, taught, by the pastors and imams, and priests of his race, and his enemies that he is a part of this society, and not an outcast. Nevertheless, everyday all around him, he sees these contradictions. He sees the inequities, in his life and the life of those around him, he see that, there is a distinct difference, in the value of his life, and those looking like him, as opposed to white peoples. No one is left anymore, to encourage him, "Up you mighty race, you can accomplish, what you will," You are the first man, to sneeze in this universe, why are you waiting on god to change your conditions? He has ignored you for more than five hundred years. In the beginning when you need the strength of god, you looked within yourselves, and look at what you've done, without help or input from anyone, why are you waiting on Jesus to come and save you, you know he has never answered, he didn't in the beginning and he won't now. Within you, and your resolve, are the answers, the same answers that caused you, to construct the pyramids. The same answers, which, caused the world, to look at you, in wonderment and amazement. You know, something is wrong, and you cannot figure out, what. The answer is simple, HEAL THYSELVES! Nothing else deserves your attention. As a man, you must provide for, and protect, your women and children, the elderly and infirmed. Every time we allow Terrorists disguised as citizen, to assault and kill us, we have that same right given to us, by the universe and the forces that produced it, to use that same power, to march them to justice. Every one of the police officer should have been dragged out, of those police stations, by black men, and given the same execution, along with their supporters. Now we have to send the message, that every time a white police officer kills an African, we are coming to get you, and introduce you to real justice. Nothing less should be expected of us, the world see and knows this, because to do so, would be to hurl an insult, at the ancestry who fought against, these injustices. (They fought as best they could, but left us in a position to fight better? They knew that actions such as these, that is descriptive of; a race of peoples is deplorable. Al. Sharpton and Jessie Jackson and Farrakhan, history will report you to be the traitors that you are. Jay z, Lil Wayne, Bill Cosby, p. Diddy, and all other notable, your distinction as collaborator, is well noted. Sadly, the black man and woman of America do not realize that, their fight for freedom are fought together, against their enemy, for their common good, not against each other. To say that the peoples named above, are race traitors, is well supported by, the fact that none, with all of their riches, has sought to change, the condition of their peoples. These peoples, the Oprah's and the likes, acts as though the ancestry behind them didn't struggles, and sacrifice, for them to be in the position that they are in. They act as though, something special, and distinct from their brethren, is attached to them. They have forgotten or they pretend to forget that they have a struggle, entirely different from our own. They are willing to settle, for assimilation, at the expense of race annihilation. They refuse to speak, on the issues of racism, and the effects of it. They do not want to disturb the status quo, they do not want to lose, or sacrifice, their gains, comforts in life. Because, they are more, informed than most of our peoples, they refuse to do what is required of them as, a privileged member of our race, the universe before it was formed gave you this privilege, It is morally correct, and right to reach back, and uplift after, you have succeeded, no other cause is greater, than your own . I don't have to say it, Just as we today look back, at the failing of those, who was privileged in history, and label them, as they should be labeled, the same will be done to all of the notable named above. It is a fact of history that, George Washington is a slave owner and a murderer, and deserves all of the honors and distinctions due one of that profession, have you not shame, you know these are the right things to teach your children. History will speak clearly on our failing. No man should bend his back for another; these are the thing, which causes wars. How great their shame must be, when they stand before the world flaunting their fame and riches. Pretending that, they are special and different. How deluded can they be? The whole world, sees your shame, everyone does, but you. When you speak, you speak on behalf of another man. You are a puppet ventriloquists, and proud to be known as such. How can you pretend that any other issue in the world deserves your attention above the present one? When given the opportunity to speak, why do you so readily show the world that, you are able to look upon your brother utter ruins and be unaffected, is it assimilation at any cost? Clearly, the world sees you as a morally unprincipled person. Stop fooling yourself you are the only one deceived. You have the world stage and you refuse to bring the issues of genocide before the world court, or you won't advocate to your brethrens, that they have the right, just as any other man, to rise up for justice. The whole world is watching, you! How can you be an advocate for the rights of humanity, when you will not stand in defense of your family, and race? Who will take you serious? You held your silence when Treyvon Martin was murder, actually, you quelled the storm, building for justice, it was you Jessie Jackson, AL. Sharpton, etc. who suppressed the will of the peoples for justice. When called upon for guidance, you had the master agenda, Why wasn't Farrakhan advocating, an Eye for an Eye, he knows the scriptures, isn't this what God requires? Why isn't all of the self-appointed black leaders, advocating in the spirit of Denmark Vesey and Nat Turner? If these leaders are not coming in the spirit of the prophets named above, they are false. Because the message brought by these prophets, is the proper answer to our problem. Why do our peoples accept mistreatment, at the hands of anyone, given our recent past? If we heeded the message of the prophets, we would not be, abused by anyone. What are you interested in protecting your personal attainments? Then it was not the peoples agenda at any point, you sold out to protect your individual attainment, none of which you would have if you would not have deceived the peoples. How can you be an advocate for the compensation of the Jew and Japanese, and not advocate for the same entitlement for your own downtrodden peoples, who endured more than four hundred years of forced labor, abuse, rape, and murder? What grips your tongue Blackman that you cannot speak in defense of yourself? These issues deserve your attention. Your children's are educated in the school system throughout the United States, and this system does not teach them that George Washington, and Thomas Jefferson, was slave owners, and so was the other so-called founding father of America. Do they teach them that when the constitution was form by these founding fathers, they did not consider the African a human being? Then you should be teaching them the truth? It is sad when a people, refuse to do what is right for themselves. Where, and who taught you, that, you need someone else approval, to do what is right for you. Why do you allow scholarships in the name of Cecil Rhode etc. to be awarded to your children's? You should be outraged at this. I do not think the ancestor would have struggled as hard, if they knew their prosperity would resign themselves to complacency. Who will tell your sons, the origin of the word Nigger, can you tell him that when the master wanted to insult the slave, he would call him nigger. Would this be a part of the truth that should be taught him, should he be taught at an early age in the schools, how he is a survival of man's worse example, of man inhumanity to man, 100 million, some historian, say as many as 200 millions, African died during the slave trade. Moreover, he is still suffering from the effects of it. Instead, you, allow him to be, taught, about how Lincoln freed the slaves. You are complicit in this mis-education of your children Black man and woman. Explain why, the men you look to for guidance, is not insisting on the restructuring of the police stations, throughout the United States? The law enforcer of these communities, should be, reflective of the communities, they are serving. Latin speaking law enforcers should be enforcing the law, in the Spanish speaking communities, and the same should apply to the black community. Black and Latin communities, has a professional class of men and women, who are capable of administrating, and, enforcing, the law; Moreover, don't they, beside white men needs employment. On the other hand, do white men only have this competence, of enforcing and administrating the law? If the above method is adopted, seemingly this would eliminated, the unnecessary killing of African men, by the Jim Bob's, of this country. We do not have to worry about the pokies of the black communities, on the police force, in the white communities killing, Wally, because there are no blacks employed, in sufficient numbers, in the white communities. It should be clear to all that, long gone, are the days when master's presence, was required for all of the slaves undertaking, we got to lay to rest, over here in the west ,the image of the Old Negro Coward. These are the challenges facing the black man everywhere, and everywhere we lack self-initiative. We sat idly by and, allowed the U.S. Government, and its agencies, to bring Cocaine, into our communities, in unprecedented amounts, and said nothing. And when the correct charges, was brought against the U.S. Government, and its agencies, by Maxine Waters and Farrakhan, they was immediately ostracized, and demonized, by the news media, and Negro leaders. They were left to fight this fight alone. No one had to agree with the Minister Farrakhan views on religion, and clearly, religion was not the issue before us, but the method employed by him was right for our communities, and us! Moreover, we should have gotten behind him, and that initiative. Beside, condemnation, did the black Christian ministers, give a better alternative? Think what our communities would be like now, if those responsible black men, was patrolling our communities, as suggested by the minister, assuredly we would not have this drug problem. (Think, if there were cooperation between the prophet Marcus Garvey, and W.e.d de-bouis, but here again ego won the day. We have to understand that it is not our agenda, but the people agenda who has appointed us to privilege. King and Malcolm should have agreed, that Violence is the opposite of Non-violence, and both was necessary for our liberation.) Nevertheless, here again the Old Slave steps forward and advocates, "Let Master (Law enforcers) Handle it" and look at their results; Prisons overcrowded, and its victim are demonized as the culprit, Why did the black churches, the Masjid, the temples, and the entertainers etc. Give the issues as raised by Maxine Water, rest! You knew that she was right when she charged the U.S. government with bringing cocaine into the community; your Sunday sermon should have talked about nothing else. It should have been in every rap song, it should have been on the lip, of every black, whose lips came in contact, with a microphone. To the pastor, and imams, you know it is morally wrong for the government of the United States, to engage in the oppression of its black citizens, you preach about Moses and the Israelite bondage. (Clearly, from the narrative, it seems that the Israelite were the victims of the Egyptians, but we know the truth,) how can you be so passionate about a fictional account of history, and hold your silence on black oppression, this makes you a hypocrite? This is the same god, you preach to the Negros about every Sunday. You applaud the fact that Moses killed that mean old Egyptian. Moreover, you want tell your own peoples that they have the same struggle. That same right is given to them by the universe, even to the point of killing, just as Moses did, to right these wrongs. If you did these things, the question wouldn't be asked; where is your merciful god, black man? Your bondage has lasted in excess of five hundred years, and look at the things you have endured. Can the fictional account, of the Israelite bondage, be in any way, compared with, yours? Where is the great compassion of this god for you? You have been praying to him, for more than five hundred years, to change your conditions. In addition, nothing has happen without your effort, and nothing will. Are you content to say that he is longsuffering? Every fiber of the universe cries out, ENOUGH! Up you mighty race you can be what you will. A man and woman, in their right state of mind, can change the impossible. Let us not get it twisted; the black preacher and imams need to teach the truth. You know in truth that the African man is the first man created of god, and this is, proven in myth and actuality. How can the Jews or any other race of peoples claim to be the chosen of god? You know that If they were god chosen, they would be the first man that he created, he was perfect. To claim anything less, is to say that god made a mistake, or that he was working with a limited amount of knowledge when he created the first man. Nevertheless, this cannot be possible with Omniscient. If the Jews, European or Arab, were the chosen of god, wouldn't god have chosen them to be his first peoples on the earth? How pathetic is their claim! The Jew, Christian, and Muslim, of being god chosen peoples. Nevertheless, this is what the Negro believes, because this is what he is taught, by his captors and the church, Temple, and Mosque. Marcus Garvey said in his book, The Philosophy and opinions of Marcus Garvey; "that the man or woman who have no confidence in self, is really an unfortunate being, and a misfit in creation" All of the so-called revealed scriptures, Judaism, Christianity, and Islam. Each claims to be the chosen of god. They are saying in essence that, God made a mistake with creating all of humanity, until he created the Jew, the Christian, and the Muslim. (To the Jews, Christian, and Moslem. can you deny the charge that you three are Satan companions? Is not everything you have done, to the African man and woman, Reflective of this? This is what the truth shows, that the injuries sustained by the African man and woman, is deliberate and calculated, and willful, and, you three are confederated in furthering, that injury. This is a shared distinction of you three; you are sons of the dens of Satan, you and your holy scriptures. Never would a God send a message or messenger suggesting the enslavement of his brethren, if he did, do not this makes him a monster, a demon?) This would preclude the need for a savior then. But the Negro don't know this, he believe still because clergy has told him so, that even though, the world have been destroyed by god for man wickedness, Man is still under the original penalty of sin. He do not know, that God, according to all three scripture, destroyed the world, because of man wickedness, and therefore, man is no longer liable for the sins committed by Adam. God, started anew, with the righteous, and Upright man, Noah. It is now suggested by the Christians in their New American Study bible, that although god wiped-out humanity, with a flood," the basic sin nature of man did not change". Nevertheless, this was the purpose of god's destruction of creation, to rid it of its imperfections. I.e. Wickedness and corruption, if these are, found in the man Noah then; theses are common attributes of humanity. Moreover, it is because of Adam, that every man has inherited it. Then how is Noah and his immediate family saved? The black man cannot and will not ask the question, "if the bible and related books is god revealed word and the above statement is true, that he destroyed the world because of man wickedness, then what need is there to send Jesus? He won't logically ask himself; what of the claims then that Jesus, was sent into the world to destroy the works of the devil, and because of Adam's sin, all men have sinned, born unto it. Neither, will he ask, these questions, of Islam or Judaism, who also claims that god, destroyed the world because of man wickedness. That means, from Adam to Noah, all sin was completely, wiped out. If that is the case then, how account for the High-sounding lies in the Qur'an, validating the sin pronouncement, against Adam? The African man and woman, under the sway of the three religions, will not ask the simple question, of the three religions why. What are man transgressions that his maker condemns him? The flood eliminated all sin and wickedness! Then why is the clergy yet teaching that, man is still under the original sin? Noah according to the narrative was a perfect man, so according to the narrative, the sin now, committed by man is at the tower of Babel. What is that sin? According to Gen.Ch.11:6,"and the Lord Said, Behold the peoples is one, and they all have one language; and this they began to do: and now nothing will be, restrained from them, which they have imagined to do. Go to, let us go down, and there confound their language, that they may not understand one another speech. Is this, man's sin after the flood? Where is the sin against god? The instructions were, given to Noah, and his descendants, to be fruitful, and multiply. RomanCh.5:12,"Therefore, just as through one man sin entered into the world, and death through sin, so death spread to all men, because all have sinned---Wasn't the wickedness found in Adam's descendants, eliminated by the flood? It was the wickedness, and corruption of man, which caused him to destroy, his creation. And. is the religious community saying, that god did not know what he was saying, or doing when he said, I will destroy the wicked, corrupt man from the earth? Moreover, that is what; he did, according to the narrative. So now, what is man sin, that he requires a savior or redeemer? Either god straightens out the problem of man sin, or he did not know what he was doing, when he flooded the earth. Neither will the African man or woman question the scripture validating the institution of slavery Exodus Ch.21:v1-11,"now these are the ordinance which you are to set before them:"if you buy a Hebrew slave, he shall serve for six years, without payment. If he comes alone, he shall go out alone; if he is the husband of a wife, then his wife shall go out with him. Further the god of the Christians ,the Jews and Muslims states "if his master give him a wife, and she bears sons or daughters, the wife and children's shall remain with the master, and he shall go out alone and Eph.Ch.6:5, "Servants be obedient to your master, in all things pertaining to the flesh". My brethrens this is the same god who came in a dream and threaten Pharaoh, because of Abraham wife Sara, and now he has a LAW STATING that " if the master gives him a wife and she bears sons and daughter, the wife and children's shall remain with the master, and he shall go out alone. Did god create man, a slave or man? Why didn't god teach his chosen peoples, the wrongs of owning another man, there is violence and abuse in that claim (ownership of another human being) and there is also shame, every nation fought again their conquerors' and enslavers surely god knows this, isn't this the reason why he intervene into the affairs of the Egyptians and Israelites? He wanted the Egyptian to let his peoples go from bondage, so that they could worship him in a place that he choose, and he knew that as long as the Israelite was in bondage, they couldn't worship him as god."No man can honor two masters at once," Jesus boasted of that fact, and yet he validated Slavery. Any practice or doctrine that does not comport with my constitution as a human being, as a man, is not right for me, this is the law that god has put in my nature and it is common to all men. Who then have the right beside the universe to strip me of it? God went to extremes to free the Israelite from bondage. Isnt, the same required of us. The forces that created us to use everything at our disposal, to right this wrong, obligate us. This is what the almighty god within us is telling us. We can end our misery and suffering under the iron oppression of the European, the Arab and the Jew, simply by doing what god requires of us. Is it, not claimed, that the Lord Jesus will come with ten thousand of his angels to, fight against Satan and his army. It does not say, that Jesus is coming to talk with Satan, Jesus is going to war!. Why is he going to War? He is going to war to right the injustices done to god's peoples and the earth. That is what the narrative say. Black Preacher and Imams, and self appointed black leaders, isn't this the things you should be teaching? The same examples Jesus will utilize when he come to right the wrongs of this world; These examples are called for now, because of the systematic killing of innocent Black men, Moses killed a Egyptian for striking a Hebrew slave, unjustly, shouldn't we be doing the same things. Christian and Muslim and Black Jew, God have given you instructions on how to behave under these conditions, why are you listening to any other god? He has told you that it is wrong to slay the innocent, and he has shown you how to behave when it happen. "And eye, for and eye", is the proper solution. Either, you believe in god laws, or you do not. Moreover, by you accepting the slaying, of innocence; clearly shows, that you do not honor gods law. You hypocrite, you worship false gods and delight in it. Moreover, you try to deceive the world into believing, that you worship, and honor I god. In your efforts to protect your agenda, you have gone so far as to condemn the innocent, simply because he is young and black. Moses, did not question, whether the Hebrew struck by the Egyptian was a thug! The only information he had was, that one of his downtrodden brothers was abused, and treated unjustly, by, the Egyptian taskmaster. This story you teach all of the time in your church, temples , and mosques, but you refuse to tell your brethren that his condition is the same as that of the Israelite, and worse! Moreover, that we are not wrong for doing exactly the same things they did to right these injustices. Look at the millions of African men young and old, the prison are overflowing with them. According to the 13th Amendment to the United States constitution, "neither slavery nor in servitude shall exist within the United States EXCEPT UPON IMPRISONMENT! You are complicit by your silence, in the enslavement of your brethren, because you know better. Hypocrite, you know that your agenda, is not gods agenda, you are a traitor to god, and you betray the spirit of the Scripture that you preach from, you are the worse of Harlot, brought by corruption for a paltry sum. Any religion or god validating slavery is demonic. By the paternal gods, my sons, respect one another, if you care to please me. For you surely, do not imagine, that you know clearly that I shall be nothing, when I have finished with my human life. For even now you have never saw my soul, but you knew its existence from what it did. And have you not seen, what terrors the souls of those who have suffered injustices bring upon the criminals; what avenging spirits they send to the evil doers And do you think the honors paid to the dead would continue, if their souls had no longer any power? I, indeed O Sons, have never believed that the soul while it is in a mortal body, lives and is dead when it is free from it: for I see that even those mortal bodies lives so long as the soul is in them. Nor can I believe that the soul will be without reason, after it has been separated from this unreasoning body; but when mind has been separated, unmixed and pure from the body, then it is likely that it will be most rational..... Consider also, that nothing is nearer to human death than sleep, and that the soul of man seems then most divine, and sees then, something of the future, because it is then most free. If these things are as I believe, and the soul leaves the body, do what I ask from reverence for my soul. But if it is not so, and the soul remains in the body and dies, even then do not do anything impious or unholy for fear of the eternal, the Omniscient, omnipotent gods, who hold together this order of all things, flawless, unfading, unfailing, and inconceivable by its greatness and by its beauty. (Xenophon introduces dying Cyrus to his children's). Thomas Paine:"I trouble not myself about the manner of future existence. I contend myself with believing, even to positive conviction, that the power which gave me existence is able to continue it in any form or manner he pleases, either with or without this body; and it seem more probable to me that I shall continue to exist hereafter, than that I should have existences as

I now have, before that existence began.... I hope for happiness beyond this life". Knowledge, of self, and self-confidence, is clearly lacking, in the African man and woman in the Diaspora. They won't trust their own judgments if it conflicts with the master position, a case in point, the African man and woman in the Diaspora will consider the prophets of every other religion, as being men of god, but not his own. They will consider, a man like Samson, as being a prophet, before they will consider, a man as great as Nat Turner, as being a prophets, Let consider the character of these prophets of the bible and related books and compare them with the prophets among the African in the Diasporas. Abraham, Married his sister; the daughter of his father but not his mother. The African man and woman want ask the question, isn't this incest? In what society, is it honored? Then how is it in the book, supposedly inspired by god? Gen.Ch.20:12,"and yet indeed she is my sister, she is the daughter of my father but not my mother, and she became my wife". This man, Abraham, as foul as he is, is revered by, the African man and woman, because he has been taught by his captors, and their slave converts (pastors, priest, rabbis, and imams) that the bible is the revealed word of god. Moreover, Abraham is the Progenitor of god chosen race of peoples, and therefore god approves. Nat turned, on the other hand, the African is taught, by the clergy, and the school system, is a criminal, because he sought to free his peoples from the bondage of the European, nations in north America. In his missions to free his peoples from slavery, Nat Stated that God lead him to this undertaking. The same as Abraham's claim that god, told him to leave his own country to a land that I will show you, and it will be an inheritance to you and your children. The African man and woman considers this true, and considers Nat turner, to be just what the captor, labeled him to be, a criminal. As well as all of the other Devine prophets, like Denmark Vesey, David Walker, Noble Drew Ali, Marcus Gravey, Booker T. Washington, Martin Luther King jr. Malcolm X, Gabriel Posey. The African in the Diaspora will not heed his message of salvation coming from his own prophets. Indeed his prophets are not prophets unless the white ruling clergy, declare him to be so. Here again the African man with no prior example of overthrowing mental slavery, you are the first man who will overcome these wretched and deplorable conditions of slavery. You are the first to reach this threshold. No Race of peoples have ever reached your depths of degradation, neither has any reached your heights of understanding. You taught the world, the true heights, that man could attain. Because you understood that, the only real and, workable god for you, were within yourself, and this fact is proven, by your first appearance here on this earth, in sub-Sahara Africa, after being the subject of your natural environment, you went within yourself, and subdued your reasoning and logic, and tamed them to your purpose. There was not any gods, outside of yourself, to solve your problems. You conquered your fears, because of your ignorance, thru reasoning and logic. Having overcome these, you left your posterity in awe, and wonderment, the whole world is in awe of you and your accomplishment, so much so that, they are saying now that aliens from out of space is responsible for your legacies, as are your posterity today, are in astonishment at your wretchedness. It is going to take you to look into yourself again, African man, and woman, to defeat this mental slavery. How can you African man, and woman say, that you Are a Jew, a Christian, or Muslim, and say that you do not believe in slavery? According to the scripture of the three named religions, the god of the scriptures sanctions slavery, and validates it. This along, should cause you to turn, from these religions, for how can you, African man, and woman, honor certain parts of a religion, and claim to be a true adherent of that religion? Ask yourself did, God freed the Israelite from bondage? According to the narrative he did, and in freeing them from bondage, god used extreme method to free them, he even killed innocent first borne babies, and divided seas, turned the river Nile into a river of blood, and during their exodus he even rained down Mania from heaven for them. Nevertheless, immediately thereafter his chosen peoples are slave-owner themselves. Ask yourselves, how is this possible? God so much abhorred slavery, that we find him complicit in escorting Moses out of Egypt because Moses had killed the awful Egyptian slave master, for this Egyptian slave master there was no protection, nothing in the universe could save the

Egyptian slaver master when the God Yahweh sent Moses to fall upon him. Why Black Man and woman Christian Muslim, and Jews, cant you ask the question, that if the above act, is an act of god, Where is this long caring and longinsuffering for you , don't you also worship, the god of Abraham, Isaac, Jacob, Jesus, Moses and Muhammad? Where is this love and compassion from this god for you? Your condition under slavery is such that it cannot be describe in words. For more than five hundred year, you have endure a form of slavery that has caused the heaven to blush, in astonishment and embarrassment, and yet you holdfast your fidelity to the gods of these religions. Black Man and woman the only God you need at this moment, is a god at hand, and he is waiting for you to acknowledge him, he has never left you, he was there before you realized that there were a you. Remember he is the god that you prostrated yourself before when facing the challenges of your environment. You Went into yourself, the only temple that god built for himself, and there met god, and left with his instructions, to overcome your conditions, of fear and ignorance. Moreover, you did, and thereafter created safety for your wife, children, and elderly, culminating, in Egypt, and luxuries and comforts. All of the facts of history came from your efforts and initiative inspire in you from God. Don't you know, that god, has never stopped inspiring you? You just stopped listening to the god in you! Who, when you witness injustice in life, tells you, this is wrong, God is telling you every day, that enslavement, murder, and rape is wrong. If, this god of the Jews, Christians, and Muslims, will not hear your complaints, About the Police murders, the unjust court system, racism, and the facts that, every nation on the face of this earth, are wagging their head at you, then you should consider, listening to the god within you, who incessantly tells you, this is wrong. He is the god that answers prayers. No god has ever required a slave, to ask his masters, to safeguard his freedom. In the story of the Israelites, god did not ask pharaoh in the narrative to treat is peoples right, he sent Moses with clear instructions, to tell pharaoh to let his peoples go. And this is the same thing, that your prophets are saying to the slaveholders around the world, Let my peoples go, so that they may worship me, in a place where I have chosen for them. This is the message brought by the Prophets Nat turner, David Walker, Denmark Vesey, Gabriel Posey, Malcolm x, Noble Ali. Elijah Muhammad, Marcus Garvey, Dr. John Hedrick Clark, Che Anta Diop. Yusuf Ben Jochanna, Martin Luther King jr. Nevertheless, repeatedly Black man and woman you reject the messages sent from your god, for your redemption telling you to change your conditions. Up you mighty race you can be what you will. Your pastors have failed you miserably, they have you worshipping at Satan alters. Telling you that, it is all right, and acceptable, on the sight god, and man; to be a slave of another. God didn't like it when the Jews was slaves in Egypt, and if he still is god, he cannot like your enslavement either. The only thing to rationalize your blind belief and faith in these religions is that subconsciously you believe the statement in Genesis, Noah pronouncement against his son Ham,(Now we know ,since it has been established that Ham is the progenitor of the African race, Ham clearly is Noah eldest son.) Curse be Canaan a servant of servant shall he be unto his brethren. "And he said, blessed be the god of Shem: and Canaan shall be his servant". God shall enlarge Japheth, and he shall dwell in the tents of Shem and Canaan shall be his servant. Is it belief in this, that has a grip on you black man, that you cannot discern the obvious? The nations holding this belief knows that, the curse pronounced by Noah has not changed, you are a servant forever, so said my God and his holy prophets and their holy scripture. Now think what is going to happen when, their so called prophet claims that your enslavement is from on high, and he can prove it by the prophets of these religion, Moses Jesus and Muhammad, the very prophets of the god you believe in, and the scriptures attributed to them. Each of these nations named above agenda is no longer hidden, because each have the same agenda, the complete enslavement of African peoples, and their scriptures exposes this fact. Look at the mercies and compassion shown to every race except you, and this is so because of Moses pronouncement against Canaan. Black man and woman, these are not the gods, you should be worshipping, you know that, this is false worship, and the God within you, are telling you, that this is not right. These gods are not real, and, He is the only, god, at hand and will answer, all of your complaints, but you must keep still, listen, and obey. Nothing produced by the universe is a mistake. Can you imagine the terrors, and the horrors, our first father, must have experienced? He was exposed to abject ignorance, in the beginning. There was not one to tell him, the benefits or the properties of lighting and thundering and rain, no one was there to tell him the benefits of these, but the god within you held you by the hand and stilled you, and gave you the answer to all of these questions. Black man and woman, he is still there, waiting on you, to visit his alters, and he yet, has extraordinary answers for you. Answers, which will, bring you, happiness, and bliss. Yes, this God is an at hand God, and he is not coming with ten thousand of his angels, to combat a situation he created. This God must come with righteousness, proclaiming that it is wrong and is an affront to reasoning and logic, to advocate the enslavement of or to enslave your fellow human, it is wrong to kill, steal, cheat, lie and take, from your fellow human, these are the law, written in the inward parts, of man, and written in his heart. Moreover, these laws are common to all men, everywhere. Any man or religions claiming something different is false, and you know that Black man and Woman, you know it to the point, that if something does not fit with your constitution, you automatically question god. If, the taking, of a new born baby, from its mother arms because, you ,want to sell it, to enrich you, and your family, if this is a grievous act to you, then, that is God in you, telling you that this is wrong. He did not, come to the priest, the imam, or the pastor to tell you that this is a shameful act, he told you at, the moment you realized that this, is a shameful act. This is the god, revealed to all men. Moreover, we should obey this one, because things said, and suggested of the god of the three religions, is wrong. I will obey nothing or anything if it is against my constitution as a human being, as a man. And to allow anyone, or anything to take, what the universe has given me, as it has given it to all other men, I cannot as a human being allow. This is my birthright! Not being the subject of another man, I am the subject of none but god, as is all other men, for I am man, and therefore I am god. The god here on this earth, and as administrator of this earth, I requires nothing from that Omniscient source, that he has not already given me. The universe provide for all living things naturally and equally. Moreover, the lessons it has taught us is, that it does not operate in, hindsight. Today makes tomorrow possible, therefore everything of today is necessary for tomorrow to be. The Omniscient God did not cause an accident in creating the man, and the universe did not produce mistakes, in manifesting him. This goes back to my initial premise, that man, the first man, is representative of God, the Absolute. This is the breath of life, which was breathe into the nostrils of man. The first man is the only man god breathes, into his nostril, and man became, a living soul according to the narrative. The life of every other man is descendant from the first man, he is not directly from god, Cain, or Abel, and they are both from Adam

and eve, according to the narrative. The first man represents absoluteness/completeness, the highs, and lows of God, the Absolute. He is the first, to experience bliss, and misery here on the earth. He is the first, to exercise godlike, understanding, here on earth, which brought him bliss, and he is also the first to lose it, which is the cause of his misery, thus, he is god on earth because, he, is the first man to experience both bliss, and misery, first. Every nation on the earth had to come, to Egypt alone the Nile, to receive their education. On religion and mathematics, medicine etc. this man did not go, to anyone else to help him, to solve his problem. He went within himself, and, found the answers, and gave them to the rest of humanity. He didn't have books to tech him on these subjects, they was given to you by the god that within you and every man, He gave them mathematic, religion, law, Planned Parenthood, Women rights, philosophy. Science, all of the discipline and the arts, originated with this man, because he dared to go within himself, to met with god, and the god within him, (that god that's common to every man,)gave him the instructions on how to, construct and shape, the reality that would bring him comfort, and contentment here in this life. He did not beg the universe to change his conditions; His very nature commanded him to change them. The same is required of you black man; there is nothing to justify you, allowing other men to over run, your communities Violating and trespassing, everything that you hold sacred. These are none other black man than, your

woman, your child, mother, and father. These are common felt sentiment, around the world, and every other man, seem to realize it but you. Ask yourself that, if your conduct here on earth, fall below the level, of that, by which we measure man, then what are you Black man? All other men, around the world, would be outrage at this, why aren't you? Are you content to see your young slaughtered in the street? Are you content to see the enslavement of your fellow African by the Arabs? Are you content to see the total destruction/ annihilation of your race? Where is there, refuge in the universe for you, claiming to be a man? No! You are not a man, you are a thing that none can name! You are a terrific pretender! Are you comfortable, that there are scriptures that you, considers sacred and infallible, that justifies your enslavement, and the enslavement of your sons and daughters? Apparently, you are because you have not acted in defense of these. Consequently, you allow your children to regard every word in these scriptures of the Jews, Christians, and Muslim, as the infallible word of god. Can you not see shame in this, these are your avowed enemies, they were from the beginning, and they remain so today with the same intent! "Cursed be Canaan, a servant of servants shall he be unto his brethren". It's in their scriptures and they believe every word of it, and this is what is taught to their children, the hand that rocks the cradle raises the nation, and the children's of these grows up believing that you will always be something less than he, no matter how wretched he or she is. You have no friends, but the god that is within you telling you daily, that this is not right. This is not just. You were noted for thousands upon thousands of years, for worshiping your woman as a goddess, how come you to regard her as a whore, how have you allowed the world to view her as such? How did you allow this to happen? It is beyond anything perverse, for you to delight in her degradation, and yet you do, and bid the world to take note! A Man you call yourself, by what measurement! God according to the scripture gave her to you, to protect her and provide for her and her children's, how is it that you have forgotten? Come out of your slumber, She needs your help, to uplift her and your children. Moreover, you claim to be a believer in these religions, you don't think that this same god requires you to stand upright, as do all other men? We are not brutes; even the primates are outraged when his woman and child are threatened! You allow your wife, children, mother father, and yourself, to pass thru the inferno fires create by other for you, consequently you are found on your knees begging a false god to rescue you. God did not put you on your knees! You did, thru your efforts, or lack of one. However, you must know black man that you are not the only one at fault here. The whole world is at fault thru their silence. If the gods of your religion are real, and he has warned you about social injustice, do you think he will applaud your folly? You have to believe that you too will find exemption from this god, as Moses did when he killed the Egyptian, and when David Had Uriah the Hittite killed for his own adulterous acts, else how account for your flagrant violation of the law of god. This god has no validity, and this is evidence by the fact, that the description of him and the examples set by him are so unjust. If there is a law against murder, in order for it to be just, it must be applied to all equally. The Jew, the Christian and the Muslim, have to be laboring under the illusion that god will excuse their behavior how else can we account for their violation of his Law; Thou shall not kill, you shall commit no adultery, you shall not steal, you shall bear no false witness against your neighbor. Remember the Sabbath day, to keep it holy, six day you shall labor and do all of your work. The seventh day is the day of the lord, in it you shall do not work. Doesn't' the three religion claim, that Ham was cursed? Moreover, his son was sentenced to perpetual slavery. How is it that god, the absolute is complicit in man enslavement. If he was god seemingly he would have acted by now, how can he hold his peace, after destroying, the entire nations of the Canaanites, Has he became frail? Again, is he complicit in their folly, or is he real? Are these lies, told of God? Clearly its, one of, the three, and if we select either, then we know that he cannot be god. That being established, leads us to the issue of Morality as it applies to the respective religious groups. Slavery is repugnant to humanity. How can you justify it and make it right, from a moral viewpoint? Is it or isn't it wrong to rape a man wife, daughter, Mother? Is it right to strip a man of freedoms given to him by God and the universe? Are not the above acts unacceptable to all of humanity? Is it Right to enslave and force peoples to work for you without compensation? Is it right to take another man wife and children, under a debt obligation? If you are saying that this is wrong according to your scripture, then what authority justify your, egregious behavior, where Your fellow human being the African is concerned? You have all contributed equally to his downfall, Judaism, Christianity, and Islam. These are the same blows, delivered by Jubalu, Jubula, and Jubulia to the head of the Master builder Harim Abiff. Where is the Wisdom, who will raise the African from his shadow grave of ignorance? In this story we clearly see that help did not come from any of the three ruffians, but it came from one higher in statute than, the three ruffian, the Help came from a king. Therefore, it is so, when it comes to raising the African from his shadow grave of ignorance, it will take a king, one possessing, wisdom. It is not, found with Moses, Jesus, or Muhammad. It will be an African man or woman, the same as their brethren. There is only one man, made from god, all other are in the similitude of this original man, so say your own scriptures, Adam and Eve are the mother and father of all other races. Therefore, there is only one king and many princes. It was the highest wisdom that raised him, and it will be this wisdom coming directly from the God within you, telling you to rise up and change your conditions, it will not happen until you do. Therefore, this Man must be you, yourself. The Jew, the Christian and the Muslim, deliberately overlooked the description given of Satan, these characteristic described of Satan are descriptive of themselves, and their activities here on earth, they have considered that the story is about them and their redemption, but clearly their scriptures are talking about fallen humanity. Moreover, Satan was, kicked out of heaven, Satan and his entourage. Judaism, Christianity, and Islam will be kicked, out of Heaven. i.e. the black man Mind. Nevertheless, it will take the god within him to direct his steps. The god honored, by Abraham, Isaac, Jacob, is demonic, and the stories told of him, shows him to be, so. The, only thing he, is offering is further misery, and Enslavement, etc. The God within you bids you to take your wife and children and rebuild your nation, The god of the scripture commands YOU, to allow the Christian, the Jews and the Muslim to, kill your children and exploit you, and use your daughters and sons as sex slaves, and you must be obedient. Further, to fill their prison houses (Slavery) with your brethren, the god within you is saying that it is wrong to allow your enemies to do so. Moreover, you have every right to do what is necessary to right this wrong. Just, as they did, in their holy scriptures. A man who, deliberately does you an injustice, is your enemy. Obey your god, within you, Jehovah, Jesus, and Allah; they are all lying to you. Proof of the fact that they are lying, is found in their own scriptures, " for in the day that you eat, you shall surely die , Adam did not die, indeed the only thing of Adam to die, that day was his ignorance, that enslaved him to his conditions. Our god, the god, within and who is common, to all men, and is known by all men, bids us to slay the ignorant Adam, and allow the conscious man to live. When Adam became conscious, he realized that God had done a phenomenal thing, because God caused him to give birth to Eve. A thing not seen in all of creation, in fact it is always the opposite, life is brought forth by the female principle, not the man, and if this was so, then Adam, as a male principle, really had something to boast! Something no other in creation could boast. Nevertheless, we know this to be not so. Even you own scriptures say as much, "Holy Mary mother of God, blest is the fruit of thy womb". So how did man give birth to Woman? She is renowned for giving birth to god, search the page of antiquity and see, if at any time, our fathers had a doctrine of man being born of man. Moreover, when you are done, searching, asks the god within you, why, in all of your human existence, have he not given you an example of man giving birth. According to the revealed scriptures, Adam, you are the only one, in creation able to do so, Even Jesus had a mother! Also, the scripture of the revealed, clearly states that God gave man dominion over everything on earth, never in the revealed scripture did he give man dominion over man, so how can you claim later, that man is subject to man's dominion! However, only one man, Ham, and his descendants is perpetually condemned to slavery, (all other men are created equal according to the U.S. constitution.) Again, any religion or god advocating, the enslavement of their fellow human is demonic, Jesus according to the narrative admonished the Israelite concerning adultery, but validated the most wretched condition, to visit humanity, Slavery! We of the human family see and agree that, slavery is the most abject state of the human being. So why, isn't your pastor, imams and rabbis, giving credence, to the fact, that contained in you bible, Quran, and the torah, are precepts, validating your enslavement by god. tell me black man and woman, what is going to happen, when a Christian Pastor, Muslim Imam, or Jewish Rabbi, claiming that, Jesus, Jehovah or Allah, requires your enslavement, and the only way to ward off god's wrath, Is to fulfill, the curse of Noah against Ham. "Curse be Canaan, a servant of servant shall he be unto his brethrens". I ask you Black Man and woman, Jew, Christian and Muslim, how can you not believe that god sanction your slavery, the New Testament, Validates it, and so do the Torah and Qur'an. You can no longer pretend, either you believe everything in these holy books or you do not. Believing part of these books will not do, you believe or you do not. Black man, and woman, you will not question the fact that, it was Noah who cursed Ham. It was not God! I want to point this out to you, because you have been, told by your Pastor, Imams, and Rabbis, that God cursed Ham, and condemned his descendants to perpetual slavery. The fact is Noah did. Ask yourself, why did god, in the beginning, give man dominion, over everything on earth except man? So where did the practice of owning another human come from: how did it find its way into god's holy word? You believe that god came down to see if Sodom and Gomorrah had done unto the call of it. Nevertheless, you do not think, reports will reach him, informing him that man, has instituted a practice of owning, another man! Seemingly, the act of owning another man would command his attention, above the sexual immorality, or social injustice for which they was accused. These are the laws given to man by god, when he departed the Ark according to the King James Version of the bible.Gen.Ch.9:1-7," and god blessed Noah and his sons, and said unto them, be fruitful and multiply, and replenish the earth. And the fear of you and the dread of you shall be upon every beast of the earth, and upon every fowl of the air, upon all the moves upon the face of the earth, and upon the fishes of the sea, unto your hands are they delivered. Every moving thing shall be meat for you; even as the green herb have I given you all things. But flesh with the life thereof, which is the blood thereof, shall you not eat. Surely, your blood of your life will I require; at the hand of every beast, will I require it, and at the hand of man; at the hand of every man's brother, I will require the life of man. Whoso sheddeth man blood, shall man shed his blood: for in the image of God made he-man. And be you fruitful, and multiply; and bring forth abundantly in the earth, and multiply therein. I therefore DARE any Christian minister, Jewish Rabbi, or Muslim imam, to show me from their scripture that the god of their scripture gave man dominion over man! Wrench come this practice of owing another man. How, did the practice of owning another human, enter into, the families, of the men, god saved from the flood? God, is showed to abhorred slavery to the point of killing, innocent baby of the enslavers! Exodus Ch.3:7, " and the Lord said I have surely seen the affliction of my peoples, which are in Egypt, and heard their cries by reasons of their task masters, for I know their sorrows; And I am come down to deliver them out of the hands of the Egyptians! This is how passionately god felt about slavery. Black man and woman, of the Jewish, Christian and Muslim, persuasion, if this was truly an act of god, aren't you entitled to this same compassion from this god? Why are you taught that someone lesser than god, gave man the authority, to have dominion over man? Moreover, you believe it! Jesus according, to the narrative honored, the curse of Noah against Ham's son Canaan, above the law's of god. Jesus knew this was wrong, but he was scared to challenge, the powers that be, for the same reasons, his father, attacked the Egyptians, and killing their first borne. Instead he validated the practice, by declaring; "Servant obey your masters in all things, pertaining to the flesh". Slavery is the reasons for god attacking the Egyptians, how does it find legitimacy among the Hebrews? This is a contradiction and it is clear to everyone. If god had chosen peoples, then clearly these peoples step from the ark. Can we at least have courage to admit this? Is Noah god? Then how does he have power to change what god considered wrong? Either we are dealing with a real god here or we are dealing with a lie. Moreover, if we are dealing with a real god, then, clearly he is a monster. If he meant for man to be the servant of man, why did he leave the urge in his nature to be something greater? Man is higher than the brute, and indeed he aspires to be greater than his station, i.e. man, he want to be god, common sense shows you that he cannot be regulated to the level of a brute, and be contented with his status. Woe be to you the Jew, Christian and Moslem, when the African man and woman has shaken off the shackle of this Mental slavery, the heaven and all of its hosts will be arrayed against you. Our struggle is on the side of righteousness. And just as you know entirely, the atrocities you committed, against your brethren, so are we aware, of your folly. An Eye for an Eye, tooth for tooth, arm for arm, and limb for limb" is god laws according to the narrative, and he never changed it. Man thru his traditions, did change the laws of god, and said god did it, Men such as Abraham, and Noah and Moses, Jesus and Muhammad. The first example set by god is the true course, and he, did not give man, dominion over man, and clearly states that, man is made in the image, and likeness of God. Therefore, Moses, Jesus, and Muhammad are liars when they claim god approves of slavery. Alternatively, they are equally lying about the reasons god attacked the Egyptians! Exodus Ch. 3:7, " And the Lord said, I have surely seen the affliction of my peoples which are in Egypt, and have heard their cry by reason of their task masters: for I know their sorrows. And I am come to deliver them out of the hands of the Egyptians". This information from the three named scriptures is proof, that Moses, Jesus, and Muhammad are fantastic liars. Moreover, their proscription for slavery is clearly their precepts, not gods. Moreover, this being the case; what does this say about Moses, Muhammad, and Jesus? Clearly, they had a stake in the trade. Jesus was outraged, at the moneychanger in the temple, but gave a law where ownership of another human being is right. He even made it a perpetual condition. Here Jesus senses failed him, because he said "man was made in the image and likeness of god", How does he have any other master? Was the slaveholder of Jesus day, a special interest group? What else can explain his position on slavery? It is clear that he acted the coward when he said" render unto Caesar, what belong to Caesar what belong to Caesar, and give to god what belong to god", as god representative here on earth he didn't have to evade that question. African Man and woman can you or any, in the world point to information that the African Prophets brought, or taught a doctrine advocating the enslavement of his fellow human. Nat Turner, didn't bring any such doctrine, neither did David Walker, Gabriel Posey, Denmark Vesey, Noble Drew Ali, Marcus Garvey, Dr John Henrick Clark, Malcolm x, dr. Martin Luther King jr, Josef Ben Jochanna, Che Anta Diop. Then why aren't you listening to them? Theirs is a message of your salvation, and it has universal application. Clearly, you can see that the god of the narrative did not intend man, to be the servant, of none but himself. This is what all of your, prophets named above are telling you? Prophet are measure by the truth they bring. Did Moses bring the truth, when he advocated the enslavement, and slaughtering of the Canaanite? God gave a law against killing. Why didn't god punish Moses, for killing? If he is, god and he meant what he said? Since he did not and he is apparently lying, because he did not punish Moses, but rewarded him with prophet hood. Look at how wicked this god is, he punished Moses for not Glorifying his name. Nevertheless, he excused the offense of murder, a sin of the first magnitude, and clearly, from the narrative, the murder of the Egyptian by Moses was willful, and calculated. Was he joking when he said, "thou shall not kill"? The Egyptians also had a law against murder, and pharaoh wanted to bring Moses to justice, but we find the god of the narrative escorting him to safety! He destroyed Sodom and Gomorrah, for sexual immorality or social injustice. Nevertheless, inherent in this statement is the fact that God charged man to be fruitful and multiply. Humankind was of one language and one mind, until God started confusion among humankind at the tower of Babel. Is the confusion, started by god among humankind, the cause of the social injustice in Sodom and Gomorrah? African man and woman, look at the evidence that showing you that this cannot be God. This is what the God within you, and who, is known by all men, he is showing you that it is all a lie! Judaism, Christianity, and Islam. Furthermore, don't you know that, you have to give god the credit for creating everything, not just qualified things, as he created Jesus, he also created Satan? I do not care what you call it, He created a good and an evil principle, and it is inherent in the nature of every living thing, in varying degrees. And so is it manifested in man, you have good and bad reasoning, and good and bad logic, and you have a good understanding about thing and a bad understanding of things, but in all, everything is representative of that Absolute Cause, that caused everything to be. Black Jew, Christian, and Muslim, Have you, asked yourself, why, the creator of everything would; require the sacrifice of animal, to atone for men sin? Is this part of the narrative a joke? Lev.6:25, "Speak unto Aaron and his sons, saying, this is the law of the sin offering: in the place where the burnt offering is killed shall the sin offering be killed before the lord: it is most holy. The priest that offers it for sin shall eat it: in the holy place shall it be eaten, in the court of the tabernacle of the congregation". Are they lying on god, why would the blood of anything be required to forgive sin? He did not apply this practice to Adam or Cain, or Moses when he killed the Egyptian. Omniscient is completely absent in the gods named above, this is descriptive of the demonic gods of our horror movies, so we know that he is an imposter, can't you see this black man and woman, the God of the Jews is no better than the God of Christianity and Islam, they are all telling the same lie! Moreover, none of them is favorable to you. Curse Be Canaan, a servant of servants shall he be unto his brethrens! It is doctrine such as these, which is the cause of your degradation, how can you remain in the ranks of believers? By what yardstick are you measuring understanding? You cannot discern the truth contained in your so-called holy books, how could you recognize god with the kind of understanding you have? You have a problem with me pointing out the fact that, it was not, god who, started slavery, it was Noah, and your own scriptures say as much. This is the message you have to point out to the world, because what if a self-proclaimed prophet of the respective religion, manifested enforcing these parts of the scriptures that you do not want to discuss in your Temple, Church, or Mosque. Will you honor the scripture or its god then? Marcus Garvey said "history is the landmark by which we are directed into the course of life. The history of a movement, the history of a nation, the history of a race is the guidepost of that movement destiny, that nation destiny, race's destiny. What you do today that is worthwhile inspires other to act at some future time. CHANCE has never yet satisfied the hopes of suffering peoples. Action, self-reliance, the vision of self, and the future have been the only means by which the oppressed have seen and realized the light of their own freedom. Life is that existence that is given to man to live for a purpose, to live to his own satisfaction and pleasure, providing that he forgets not the god who created him and who expects a spiritual obedience and observation of the moral laws that he has inspired. There is nothing in the world, common to man, that man cannot do. The ends you serve, that's selfish will take you no further than yourself, but the ends you serve, that are for all, in common, will take you even into eternity. Its god is only the belief, and the confidence, we have in a god, why man is able to understand his own social institutions, and move, and live, like a rational human being. Take away the highest idea; faith and confidence in a god, and mankind at, large are reduce to savagery, and the race destroyed. A race without authority and power is a race without respect. Criticism is an opinion for good or ill, generally indulged in by the fellow who more than anyone else is indulge yet, the biggest fool period. There is no criticism that call not forth yet another. The last critic is the biggest fool of all. For the world starts and end with him. He is the source of all knowledge, yet knows nothing, for there is not, a word, one find to use that there not another, that hath the same meaning, then wherefore do we criticize. Listen to these words from this African woman back then; they are the same voices, speaking now. Excerpts from a book entitled, Incident in the life of a slave girl; by, Linda Bren (Harriet Jacob,). "The first years of my service in Dr Flint's family, I was accustomed to share some indulgencies with the children of my mistress. Though this to me, seemed no more, than right. I was grateful for it, and tries to merit the kindness the faithful discharge of my duties, but I was now entering on my fifteen year--- a sad epoch in the life of a slave girl. My master began to whisper foul word to my ears, young as I was, I could not remain ignorant of their import. I tried to treat them with indifference or contempt. The master, age, my extreme youth, and the fear, that his conduct would be, reported to my grandmother, made him bear this treatment for many months. He was a crafty man and resorted to many means to accomplish his purpose. Sometimes he had stormy, terrific ways that made his victim tremble; sometime he assumed a gentleness that he thought must surely subdue. Of the two, I preferred the stormy moods, although they left me trembling, he tried his best to corrupt the pure principles my grandmother had instilled. He pictured my mind with unclean images, such as only a vile monster could think of. I turned, from him with disgust, and, hatred. But he was my master. I was compelled to live under the same roof with him—where I saw a man forty years my senior daily violating the most sacred commandments of nature. He told me that I was his property; that I must be subject to his will in all things. My soul revolted against the mean tyrant. But where could I turn for protection? No matter whether the slave girl be as black as ebony or as fair as her mistress. In either case, there is no shadow of law, to protect her from insults, from violence, or even death; all of these are inflicted by the fiends, who bear the shape, of men. the mistress, who ought to protect the helpless, victim has no other feeling toward her but those of jealousy and rage, The degradion, the wrong, the vice, that grows out of slavery, are more than I can describe, they are more than you would willingly believe. Surely if you credited half the truth you are told countless millions suffering in this cruel bondage, you at the north would to help to tighten the yoke. Refuse surely would refuse to do for the master, on your own soil. The , mean and cruel work, which trained bloodhounds, and the lowest, class of whites do for him at the south. Even where the years brings to all enough of sin and sorrow. But in slavery, the very dawn of life, is darken by these shadows. Even the little child, who is accustom to waiting on her mistress and her children, will learn before she is twelve years old, why it is that her mistress hates such and such among the slaves, perhaps the child mother is among those hated. She listen to violent out breaks of jealousy passion, and cannot help understanding what is the cause. She will become prematurely knowing in evil things. Soon she will learn to tremble, when she hears her master footfall. She will be compelled to realize that she is no longer a child. If god had endowed beauty upon her, it will prove her greatest curse. That which commands admiration in the white woman only hastens the degrading of the female salve. I know that some are too much brutalize by slavery to feel the humiliation of their position; but many slaves feels it most acutely, and shrink from the memory of it. I cannot tell how much I suffered in the presence of these wrongs, nor how I am still pained by the retrospect, my master met me at every turn, reminding me that I belong to him, and swearing by heaven and earth that he would compel me to submit to him. If I went out for a breath of fresh air, after a day of unwearied toil, his footstep dogged me, if I knelt beside my mother grave; his dark shadow fell on me even there. The light heart nature had give me, became heavy with sad foreboding. The other slaves in my master's house notice the change, many of them pitied me, but none dares to ask the cause. They had no need to inquire; they knew too well the evil practice under that roof. And they knew that to speak of them was an offense that never went unpunished. If god is god and, and he did intervene into the affairs of the Egyptians, on behalf of the Israelites. The acts described herein should have made him kick over heaven and earth. How could he hold his peace? The evidence shows, that the slave girl Linda Bren has more moral and compassion than this god of Abraham, Moses, Jesus, and Muhammad. Even in her most evil moments, she considered other women in her situation, why didn't the god of the Jews, Christians or Muslim, answer her? He allowed this to go on and did nothing. The very acts described above, make demons and devils blush, God would never approve! Nevertheless, this is the message expounded upon by all of the named prophets of Judaism, Christianity, and Islam. They were devil, worshipping demons then, and they remain so today. How can you not see this black man and woman? This is how the American public and the European nations, know that you do not know your history because if you did, you could never form a relationship, or association, with him on a human level. Even though they bear the form of man, there the similarity ends. Am I speaking extreme radicalism? This is beyond extreme, and the pages of history, your footprints, (clearly cut,) which all can see, and know that truly this is your legacy. I use to think that Elijah Muhammad, and others who labeled whites as devil was extreme, but after searching the pages of history, and realizing the things you have done, European, Jew, and Arab, what other name is there for you? If this was your behavior in the past, I could accept it more readily. Nevertheless, your behavior has not changed. If it had, you have had more than enough time to straighten out your educational system, you would teach the whites the truth about man origin, where civilization started and how it transferred to the rest of humanity. Everyone story should be told. You would be outraged, at the unjust killing of African men. You would stop the unjust imprisonment of black men; you would give no man in this society, rights above another. Absent this, we who think as we ought to think, know that the message brought by, you, Moses, Jesus, and Muhammad, is demonic and is not worthy of human attention. I know that information such as this offends you, but if you are offended by this truth, then you should have these feelings anyway. The things done to the African and woman ought not to have been done, to a human being. Useless you have the morals and consciousness of a demon. If there was an effort, on the part of the three religions, Judaism, Christianity, and Islam, to right these wrongs, it could be, argued that, these religions, prefer good to evil. How can any of name religions, speak on morality knowing the things, they have done to the African man and woman. The Rabbis, the Pastor, or the Imams will not teach this. Because they are, retained liars, and to say otherwise, would condemn their religious faith. Therefore, they remain as stated, demon devil worshippers. But you black man and woman, can change your conditions, listen to what the god within you is saying to you, look at the shame in the words you just read, and the comparison made, is there fault with the things I have said in the pages above? Then follow the god who is telling you that this is wrong, no other god, deserve your attention! He is showing you when to act, on these things and how. It is not, right. In fact, it is outrageous, and downright insulting to sit back, and watch your women folks assaulted. And you do nothing, you are totally unfeeling, that a white racist masquerading as a police officer dragged this black woman,(the world is satisfied with seeing it also, because who has shown outrage.) while she was dead. Moreover, you know he murdered her, but you are satisfied to let your enemies, tell you, something happen that you know, is not true. Haven't you had your fill of their lies? Then why are you listening to anyone other, than the god within you and all men, you know he is not lying. Nevertheless, you know that Muhammad is lying, in the Qur'an. In Sura 16 Ayat 89,"one day we shall raise from all peoples a witness against that people, and we shall bring you O Muhammad, as a witness against these, your peoples. There is a footnote immediately below this chapter, which states that Allah will raise from all peoples a witness against those peoples, speaking their language, and the prophet, Muhammad will be a witness against the Arab peoples. How can he claim in the same Quran that he is the seal of the prophets, and the last prophet to the world? African man and woman ask yourself, how can he be a witness against the African in the Diaspora, who does not, speaks the Arabic language. (If the Torah, was god's reveal word, what need is there for the bible. And if the bible is god 's revealed and inspired word, what is the need for the Quran? If the corruption of the Torah, precipitated, the need for the bible, couldn't he, as god divine what would happen with the Quran? Each validates ownership of another human, which shows the corruption of the three, "Man is made in the image and likeness of God" there is no other master of his in the universe.) A Denmark Vesey, or one of the African prophets, in the Diaspora, fit the description of a witness against us? Can't we at lease have the courage to admit that, according to the Qur'an, Muhammad cannot be the seal of the prophets? Moreover, are we to believe that Muhammad flew from Medina to Mecca on a carpet? Don't you see how ridiculous this sounds? Nevertheless, these fantastic lies are, found in the scriptures of the revealed religions! Moreover, they claim, that it was, revealed, of god. Well the god within all of us is saying that this is a blatant lie, all of it. Moreover, you are proud to have you child learn the Arabic language, because it is also stated in the Qur'an that Arabic is the most beautiful of language. At some point, you must realize the error of your ways. Why not, teach him his African tongue, Why not the Egyptian language? Why do you allow you sons to be athletes at the colleges? Don't you know that the athletics programs at the school are modern day slave systems? You allow your sons and daughters to get into career threatening sports, in which the school get millions of dollars from their efforts, and they get nothing, for four years, and if he is injured, he is laid out to pasture, just as the old slave. He made all of this money for the school, and he is entitled none of it. Just as the slave worked from Sun up to sun down and was entitled to nothing. Shame on you black man, why do you pretend that you do not see this? Why do you go to the temple, the church, and the mosque, and give these peoples your money? Don't you realize that they owe you money? They are the very one's behind your enslavement, their prophets and their god. Go and search the pages of history, and see exactly what role the Catholic Church, and the protestant, the Jews and Muslims, played in your enslavement. Moreover, they are yet involved in it, all of them. Then you will see, how degrading, and humiliating slavery is. The raping, of women and the killing of innocence; reduces man, to the level of a brute. White man, and Jew and, Muslim, there is nothing in the above acts to boast! They are the worse acts committed in the universe, but this is your legacy, is this the reasons why you won't include it in your history books? Is this the reason why you do not teach it in your Temple, church or mosque? Is it because you know the world will see the shame in your acts? The three of you have the same temperament, different from the African, history shows your first appearance on the world stage, and it is one of barbarity. The African temperament is more humane, as is evident, in his societies, and his exchanges with all of humanity. This is your legacy. In the African societies, the woman was exalted to mans equal, whereas in Europe she was a liability, if she was told to get out by her man, she perished. Because no one else would take her in, she was another mouth to feed. Europe, at this time had, only three month to gather, and harvest food for the year. In addition, they practice polyandry, one woman to five men. She could, be beaten, at any time and discarded or killed, at anytime. In European societies, she was merely a beast of burden. Go and search the pages of history and see for yourself, how the women of Europe was treated, during their emergence from the ice. Moreover, look at the law of Hammurabi, in these laws of the west, what is moral about these laws? They made it a law that a slave could be beaten with a stick, but only of a certain size, is this supposes to make it morally right, to own another human being? Is this humane! Moreover, in Islam a woman could be beaten with a stick of a certain size, and refuse food until she obeyed. Is there anything humane about these acts? In addition, in Christianity, the woman cannot even speak in church, if she wants to be heard in church, she must speak thru her man. What is humane about any of your acts? Only in the African societies and their religion, was the woman exalted, even to the station above god, we made her the Mother of god. The very god concept came from the African man and woman of the Nile valley. Moreover, the goddess was the first god to be worshipped by man. Therefore, black man and woman, given your conditions and situation, clearly you are moving thru life with another man idea, and the proof I offers to support my contentions is, the African always esteems his woman with high regards, and treated her as an equal. The Jew, the Christian, and the Muslim, concept of fairness is wrong and belong among uncivilized peoples. You do not worship god black man and woman, you worship another man ideal. You are the worse, of fakers, you believe what you want too, from these scriptures, and think that you are a true adherent. If you do not believe, in the slavery expounded upon in these books, then you are faking, how can you believe some of the things, said of god and his holy books, and not believe all of it? "A servant of servant shall he be unto his brethren. These precepts have not changed, so do not complain when the law is executed against you, and you find yourselves, once again enslaved! Look at your conditioning, you are more than 80% of the prison population here in America, Your is five time the rate of china, and all of the countries of Europe combine don't have this ratio. These are your sons and daughters black man and woman; you know that this is slavery? Can't you see the vast difference, in the sentences given to black offenders and white one? Why is it, in most of the courtrooms, there is a white judge sitting in judgment on your sons and daughter? You know as well as I, that we have competent judges who are capable of interpreting and enforcing the law, and yet you sit back and allow these wrong doing and say nothing. These are things, we should be demanding, which is no more than right. Every chance they get, they send one of our sons, or daughter to what they know, is slavery (prison). Then you will see that Jim bob will not be getting away, with so many black killing. You have to stop pretending that these things are not happening. There is a simple solution to these problems, we don't need a white overseer, to administer our affairs, and the white power structure needs to understand this, and if they are hesitant in complying, then they should be forced to comply, we have every right in the universe to effect this. We have allowed this to go on for much too long. It is time now to look at things correctly. The white power structure, wants to tell your story, of enslavement. They teach you, and your children's, that slavery for you, ended in 1865. Moreover, they purposely omit, the terrorist acts that soon followed, the removal of the physical shackles. They, teach these false hoods, and you allow their teaching, to become the official teaching of your children's, consequently you can't, and won't teach him, about the thousands of black men lynched, between 1880 and 1930, an estimated 2,400 black men, women, and children were killed by lynch mobs. A partial list of crimes, included gambling, quarreling, arguing with a white man, being accused, of raping, a white woman, or speaking inappropriately to one etc. this has happen, black man and woman, just recently, and you have forgotten, and consequently we have a modern version of lynching now. The African man or woman will not make it to the police station, to be dragged out, and lynched. With this modern version, he (the African) will be, executed on the spot. Moreover, you allow this to happen, but still, you are not outraged. You should never give anyone the rights, to do things to you that you cannot, do to him. Look, at the things your religion has caused you to accept, you know it is not right. Yet you get on your knees and pray for that poor Jesus, who was, crucified by those cruel men! You have forgotten, because you have allowed others to teach you that your misery, (slavery ended in 1865), and you have neither courage to ask yourself, what kind of slavery was it after 1865 until the present. They want to silence you, on the lynching that took place, these acts of man against man, are the most vicious acts imaginable, and they took pictures to prove what I am saying. They are truly disturbing; disturbing to the point that you, black man cannot bear, to look at them. They are showing you, in your face, what they did to you and your peoples. Moreover, you refuse to fix your gaze to see. They have museums showing, how they ravaged your women, and killed your sons and daughters, and, to add insult, to injury, they parade you, around the world, showing the world what they have made of you, a thing which none can name! One who will kill anyone, or anything, except his master? Is this a man, black man? It is time to bring master's ass to task, for all of the wrongs you have done, and you continue to do. These pictures are so graphic and they tell chilling horrors stories, stories that shock the consciousness of any moral being. There are whole families hanged, and the white population, are standing around, eating hotdog, and posing for fashion. This just stopped happening in the 1950's, and now we have a new phase. This time, it is the police out front, instead of the mob, and look at their rationale, He, resisted, I feared for my life, etc. just as then, do these acts justify the killing of African peoples? You know it do not, black man, as well as I, and the world know it to. When they lynched, a African man, and gave the reason for his hanging, we knew they was lying, when they said he talked backed to a white man, but even if he did, it still did not justify the whole white community rising up and lynch a man because of his opinion, because he agreed or disagreed. Nevertheless, just as then, we are wrong, if we allow this to happen and do nothing. if we accept the systematic killing of our peoples, and wait on the law enforcer, or Jesus, or Allah, or Jehovah, to stop it, we was looking, for that same kind of justice, back then, from the sheriff, and other law enforcer, and of course Jesus and the other gods mentioned above. We know what happen next, as soon as the police got there, they let him go. Moreover, they are still allowing them to go. and the sad thing is, we know they are. They took this racist white boy to burger king after killing nine black peoples in a church. You have got to stop listening to you master opinion, he is contented with the status quo, and if we just let this blow over, we can all have peaceful and happy lives, Jessie and Al, and Louis. We have to let the judicial system work. These so-called leaders never stopped to think, on the advice given by the master. Do you think that, he will advise you, on how to remove his Yoke? Alternatively or how to implement measures that will destroy the peace and stability of his home. He is not willing to compromise his comforts for your struggle. Moreover, we know that, so we should be listening to no other god, than him within us that, see the truth in the conclusion we have drawn. We have no friends in white America, and we do not have a friend in Jesus, Jehovah, or Allah. Jesus is not the kind of savior we need, too long we have followed his example, he willingly crawled upon that pole as god, and allowed the Jews, and Romans, to do the things, they did to him. Moreover, we have followed his examples and laid down, and allowed the Jews and the Roman and, the Arabs, to do all of these ungodly things to us. Why do we believe in this Jesus? Don't you know, from your own bible, and Qur'an, that he reneged, on every promise he made, to the peoples listening to him? "For verily I say unto you, that no man, standing here today, shall taste of death, until the son of man, comes in his glory". You black man and woman know as well as I, that all of those peoples are dead. Moreover, none received any of the riches, houses, mother, sons or daughters, in this life as JESUS promised. Ask yourselves why would, he tell such fantastic lies? In addition, why would anyone believe him, he could not save himself. No one have saw him since his crucifixion, and if we believe he has made other showing, they are not frequent showing, he too, black man and woman, must be afraid of the Romans and the Jews. I cannot believe that he has held his peace, Jesus or his father, about this slavery issue. "And that slave, who knew his master will and did not get ready or act in accord with his will, will receive many lashes. But the one, who did not know it, and committed deeds worthy of a flogging, will receive but few", Luke Ch.12:47. Here you have the savior of humanity validating the most egregious practice in the universe. The god who is within us all is much more moral, and he condemns the practice. So compare, who is god, and who is devil? The one who condemns slavery, or the one who validates it? By the way, Jesus, you have the Negro right now standing around, two thousand years after the fact, waiting on you to come in all of your glory. To fight his battle that he should be fighting for himself. Your savior Jesus, black man and woman would not, fight his own fight. How can you have faith that he will win yours! He won't win this fight With the turn, the other cheek strategy, and it don't logically seem that he will employ that strategy, because he is suppose to be coming with ten thousand of his angels, to destroy the works of the devil. Ask yourselves black man and woman, if that is what he is going to do, then why would he leave you with a turn the other cheek doctrine? Why would he advocate these measures, knowing the pain and misery it causes? Moreover, you see, from the narrative that he did not come, to free the slave from his conditions, rather he came to perpetuate it. So why are you waiting on him? For what, to tell you, how much longer you must, be a slave? Seemingly, black man and woman, you do not want to go to Jesus heaven, because you will be a servant there also. It's the same as the slave with a lot of money, and his relation with the master, the fact that he has money does not elevate him to the master's level, he remains a slave to the master, and he won't let the slave forget it, so he knows that his sitting is naturally, in the servant quarters. Jessie, Al and Louis, can tell you all about this, but don't listen to them, because they are silver tongue liars, just watch what they do. They are not screaming genocide, and nothing but genocide! They are not saying, up in arms Black man, and woman; this is your birth -rite, to defend yourself. These we know they are fake! "The man that stands up on the corner of the path, and points the way, but does not go is just a pointer, and a block of wood can do the same. The teacher leads the way, on every span of ground, he leaves his footprints clearly cut, which all can see, and be assured that he their master went that way. Denmark Vesey, Gabriel Posey, David Walker, Malcolm X, Nat Turner, Diop, Dr. John Henrick Clark, Yusuf Ben Jochanna, Ian Van-Sertima, Marcus Garvey, Noble Drew Ali, George Jackson, etc. These masters' teachers and prophets left these footprints, which all can see, and be, assured that, this is the way to go. Now for Jessie, Al, and Louis, to come preaching a different message, then we know you are not true. How can you (Jessie, Al, and Louis, after perusing the pages of history, and realizing what you have learned, about what the nations of Europe, and its peoples have done to us as a peoples,) be so nonchalant about this. You was aware long ago, that these peoples have museum, on our lynching, you should have never allowed those images, to be remote, in the minds of our peoples, you should have mentioned, in everything you wrote, something about those, lynching. How can you not be alarmed and outrage at the possibility, that African children are being kidnapped, and their organ stolen, to be sold on the black market. You know you should be paying attention, for our children's, sake. Look at the thousands, of black children, who are, reported missing and never seen again. This is not just happening in America, but around the world, these African children are being abducted, and their organs sold to the highest bidder. Why you haven't placed this issue before, the African public? Why do you have an agenda with Master's, beside the ones confronting us as a race of peoples? They are not going to compromise their principles for you, so why are you compromising, yours as a man? Aren't you at all ashamed of your behavior, as a man? aren't you at all concerned with what we, and your posterity think of your actions, How can you Jessie, Al, and Louis, after seeing those pictures, not only of our lynching here in the States, but you were aware of these atrocities committed by the nations of Europe against African peoples worldwide, and you still advocated a doctrine of inclusion? You knew better than most of our peoples that we have no friend in the European, the Arab, and the Jew. The acts committed against us by these nations, ought not, to been done to any human, No human with morals, can commit these horrors! There is another name however, for such peoples. Moreover, they are commonly, called demons and devils. Your diabolical act, since your appearance on the world stage, describes you as such. This is the reality, the African man, must come to, in order to defeat his mental bondage. You have been, brutalized so long under these conditions, until you cannot tell that you are actually ill. Proof of the fact that you are ill, is your constant rationalization, of your conditions, and it is showing you, all day, and every day, that you cannot go through life, with your head up as a man pretending, to be a man. however, you won't listen to him. You know better than, all, of the races, that you cannot be a man, under these conditions, even pretending.

Plate 31
Marion, Ind
Aug. 1930.

WHAT IS THERE LEFT TO SAY BLACK MAN

COPYRIGHT - 1911 - G.H.FARNUM
OKEMAH, OKLA

WHAT IS THERE LEFT TO SAY BLACK MAN

"The Riots in New York: The Mob Lynching a Negro in Clarkson Street." (*Illustrated London News*, August 8, 1863)

Levi's

Authorities'

Dr. Yusuf Ben Jochanna, Africa the Mother of Civilization, The Black man of the Nile his family, The African origin of the major western religion religions,

Dr. John Henrik Clarke, African peoples in world history, who betrayed the African world revolution.

Ian van Sertima, African presence in early Europe, and the African presence in early America.

Che Anta Diop, Civilization, or Barbarism, the cultural unity of black Africa. Black Africa.

David Walker, David Walkers Appeal.

Marcus Garvey, the philosophy and opinions of Marcus Garvey

Noble Drew Ali, the holy Koran of the Moorish Science Temple of America,

Chancellor Williams, the Destruction of Black Civilization,

Gerald Massey, the Natural Genesis, a book of the Beginning, The Historical Jesus, and mystical Christ

Albert Churchward, sign and symbols, of primordial man, the origin and evolution of the Human Race, and the origin and evolution of religions.

Count C.F.Volney, ruins of empires,

Kersey Graves, the world sixteen crucified saviors

The King James Bible

The new American standard bible

The Holy Qur'an, Yusuf Ali, Version

www.ingramcontent.com/pod-product-compliance
Lightning Source LLC
Chambersburg PA
CBHW060430290526
45791CB00002B/917

* 9 7 8 1 5 1 6 9 7 2 5 9 3 *